LEAN STONE PUBLISHING

"Turn the Page And Live a Better Life"

www.leanstonebookclub.com

© Copyright 2017 Lean Stone Book Club - All rights reserved.

In no way is it legal to reproduce, duplicate, or transmit any part of this document in either electronic means or in printed format. Recording of this publication is strictly prohibited and any storage of this document is not allowed unless with written permission from the publisher. All rights reserved.

The information provided herein is stated to be truthful and consistent, in that any liability, in terms of inattention or otherwise, by any usage or abuse of any policies, processes, or directions contained within is the solitary and utter responsibility of the recipient reader. Under no circumstances will any legal responsibility or blame be held against the publisher for any reparation, damages, or monetary loss due to the information herein, either directly or indirectly.

Respective authors own all copyrights not held by the publisher.

Legal Notice:

This book is copyright protected. This is only for personal use. You cannot amend, distribute, sell, use, quote or paraphrase any part or the content within this book without the consent of the author or copyright owner. Legal action will be pursued if this is breached.

Disclaimer Notice:

Please note the information contained within this document is for educational and entertainment purposes only. Every attempt has been made to provide accurate, up to date and reliable complete information. No warranties of any kind are expressed or implied. Readers acknowledge that the author is not engaging in the rendering of legal, financial, medical or professional advice.

By reading this document, the reader agrees that under no circumstances are we responsible for any losses, direct or

indirect, which are incurred as a result of the use of information contained within this document, including, but not limited to,
—errors, omissions, or inaccuracies.

New Age, Bundle 2
Astral Projection, Lucid Dreaming

Table of Contents

ASTRAL PROJECTION 6
Introduction 7
Chapter 1 – Historical References of Astral Projection 10
Chapter 2 - What Exactly Is Astral Projection? 16
Chapter 3 - How Does It Happen? 19
Chapter 4 – How Can You Travel the Astral Plane? 23
Chapter 5 - Understanding the Benefits of Astral Projection 36
Chapter 6 - Can Astral Projection Be Dangerous? 41
Conclusion 43

LUCID DREAMING 44
Introduction 45
Chapter 1 – What is Lucid Dreaming? Understanding Lucid Dreaming, the Process, and Format 47
Chapter 2 – Why Would You Want to Have Lucid Dreams? 53
Chapter 3 – How Can You Have Lucid Dreams? 58
Chapter 4 – How Can You Stimulate Lucid Dreaming or Assist Lucid Dreaming via Technology, Drugs, or Supplements? 63
Chapter 5 – What Is It Like to Dream Lucidly? 66
Chapter 6 – How Do I Control My Dreams? 72
Conclusion 78

Astral Projection

The Complete Guide for Beginners on Astral Projection, and How to Travel the Astral Plane

Introduction

PROBABLY THE BEST BOOK CLUB ONLINE...

"If you love books. You will <u>love</u> the Lean Stone Book Club"

*** <u>Exclusive Deals</u> That <u>*Any*</u> <u>Book Fan Would Love!</u> ***

Visit leanstonebookclub.com/join

(IT'S FREE)!

This book contains proven steps and strategies on how to experiment and have an unbelievable out of body experience through astral projection.

You've surely heard or read at least once about people confessing how, through a near death experience or under the influence of hallucination-inducing drugs, they have traveled outside their body. Or about how their dreams or meditation trances are so intensely vivid that they are capable of feeling and living things that can't be physiologically explained. Regardless of what you have heard before, you've surely wondered if such experiences are actually possible, and if they occur randomly or could be willingly induced. Well, in this book, you will find the precise responses to these questions, and much more.

Since the dawn of time, humans have wondered whether the source of self awareness resides in their bodily form, or is associated with a defined entity only sheltered in it. The existence of spirit has long been debated, but hypotheses and practices that sustain and confirm it abound in veridical details. From real life stories, to religion, culture, and literary works of fiction, a distinction between the physical body and the spiritual body has been clearly made. So, while the first exists solely in the material dimension, the latter can travel outside of it, in its own astral world or astral plane.

Astral projection consists of detaching your spiritual form from the bodily one, and going to places that you could not normally or easily access. Earthly places, but spatial too. In a way, it is a flying and floating activity that allows you to explore a world beyond mundane reach. It is a truly magical adventure you too can embark on after going through this comprehensive guide.

So, if you are eager to connect to your deepest nature, and probe the sense of powerfulness of being in touch with your metaphysical self, look no further. The purpose of this book is to help you better grasp the essence of your life psyche. Moreover, the possibility to astrally project your spiritual body indirectly suggests the verity of life after death claims. What could be more amazing than the idea of implicit eternity? However, you must be aware that astral projection is not recommended for people that suffer from psychological disorders or related issues, as it could impair their distinction between real experiences and out of body occurrences. Other than that, it is a safe and harmless path you can choose to follow in order to better the quality of your life.

Chapter 1 – Historical References of Astral Projection

The practice of astral projection can be tracked throughout history thousands of years ago. The concept of acquiring knowledge, enriching personal culture, and enhancing the religious bond with deities through an out-of-body experience (OBE) is clearly explained in various manuscripts and artistic works across many nations. Regardless of the meaning associated with it, the actual travel in astral planes is primarily seen as a valuable step in enlightening and self-awareness.

Inquisitiveness is an innate feature of our species' nature, so it is not surprising that people have always sought to discern a higher significance for living, one that transcends the mortal shell. Based on personal encounters, imaginative exercises, or others' accounts, some people managed to accurately describe the process of spiritual walking or soul travel that astral projection in fact embodies.

Succinctly described below are the most relevant documentations about astral travel that hundreds of generations have produced and passed on from ancient times until present time.

1. Religious doctrines and cultures

The most overwhelming presence of astral projecting implementation can be noted when it comes to the various faithful ideologies manifested across the Earth. The importance of spiritual travel pervades many symbolic representations in cultural lifestyles too, and is not less remarkable in creative reproductions. In fact, anthropological studies have estimated that the majority of cultures that populated the Earth at different times believed to a certain degree in the occurrence of this immaterial experience.

Ancient Egypt - Some claim that the oldest references to astral projection can be found in ancient Egyptian manuscripts. Moreover, it is believed that the great pyramids have been built to facilitate it. Egyptians differentiated five components of the human soul. One of them was Ka, the vital substance or the spirit, which could leave the body at will and travel. However, when the person died, Ka was trapped inside the tomb. Another part was Ba, which could travel the mortal world only after death and venture into the Underworld. Ba kept returning to the tomb until it was possible, when the time came, for it to reunite with Ka in the afterlife.

Chinese Culture - The ancient Taoist religion has been among the first to formulate the idea of a divine self. One meditative practice involves drawing in and focusing the energy spread inside the body, and channeling it to be able to travel and be in different places at the same time.

Indian Religion - In centuries old scriptures of Hinduism, and in Purana texts, it says that magical powers, named Siddhis, can be achieved through meditative and Yoga exercises. One of them, mentioned in the Bhāgavata Purāna is the capacity to undergo astral travel, known as manaḥ-javah, one of the ten secondary Siddhis. There are descriptions of miracles performed through astral projection in the Hindu religion.

On the other hand, Buddhism promotes a principle of reincarnation, where not a clearly defined soul, but a consciousness flow, travels from one life to another in time. However, astral projections in a dream-like state are recalled in this religious doctrine too, as the faithful individuals assumingly can establish a bond with Buddha in an astral plane. There are stories that relate how monks can travel to various levels of heavens, using this form of teleportation, through intense focus and self-discipline.

Roman Empire - The belief that the human spirit is created of a special, unearthly matter, just like the one the stars are made of, was pretty common among many sects in the Roman times, and it was adopted into early Christianity too. Experiences of astral travel displayed in divine visions, and appearances in people's dreams are often mentioned in documents dating back to those times.

In addition, some people believe that certain passages in the Bible make clear suggestions to spiritual travel. It is thought that a high level of devotion, expressed through prayers and strict rites, can help to establish a connection with the astral plane, which is perceived as the place where angels, demons, and other entities exist.

Native Americans - Many tribes of Native Americans also sustained a doctrine of reincarnation and astral projection, noticed by the first travelers in the New World. The so called shamans were the ones who held the secrets of this practice, and they apparently used it to localize herbs used for healing, and find the best places to settle in across the landscape, and to foresee events.

2. *Philosophy and Occultism*

From Plato to Socrates, Pliny, and Plutarch, dreams and experiences that correspond to astral travel have been extensively recorded. The early thinkers and founders of the Western philosophy have expressed their preoccupation with afterlife in their works and mystical views related to the soul and its place in the corporeal reality.

The astral plane is perceived as a middle world of light, between Heaven and Earth, and populated by angelic or demonic entities in philosophical systems popular during the Renaissance, such as Theosophy and Hermeticism. The astral bodies are considered to be components of this plane, and the astral or spiritual body, made of light too, has the role of bonding the physical body to its rational double.

Considered an occult experience by many, in traditions associated with occultism, astral travel is accessed through controlled visualizations and breathing exercises. Often hypnotic-like states and mental representations of a secondary body are used, and the sense of awareness is then voluntarily transferred there.

3. Literature and Art

Prose and Poetry - Many fiction, nonfiction books, and poems have been written about the fascinating subject of astral traveling, but probably the most popular are Dante Alighieri's poetry book, *Divina Commedia*, and Honore de Balzac's fictive work, *Louis Lambert*.

In the last few decades, lots of biographical books relating out-of-body experiences, which initially occurred through near death experiences after surgical interventions or involuntarily, have become available to the public.

Painting - Contemporary exhibitions of astral travel represented on canvas are not ordinary, but not very unusual either. Also, nowadays, a multitude of designs illustrating the individual's journey through this spiritual experience are available online, as paintings or images imprinted on various accessories.

Music - Trance inducing music played with a flute has also been used by Native Americans to facilitate the process of astral projection, and in current times, meditation music is quite common and also sought for the very same purpose. There is also an Israeli band, named Astral Projection that produces a so called psychedelic trance type of electronic music.

4. Modern Science

There are controversial and contradictory statements when it comes to scientifically proving a solid base for astral projection, as many studies and experiments have had various outcomes. While some argue that an out-of-body experience's authenticity can't be determined with practical instruments, and label it as a dream state, others state the opposite and use as evidence the knowledge gathered through psychic means, and the consistent incidence of such cases. Statistically, millions of people have claimed to have lived conscious out-of-body experiences. It has been estimated that one person in ten experiments with it at least once throughout their life.

Out of numerous studies, there are two worthy of mentioning. Their outcomes reinforce indirectly, but indubitably the genuine existence of astral projection occurrences, or at the very least, the actual soul's very state.

In the first research study, a neurologist, Dr. Henrik Ehrsson, used equipment to induce out-of-body experiences and the participants confirmed it. In this particular experiment, screens were placed over the participants' eyes. These screens transmitted images recorded live by cameras placed behind the participants. When the researcher uses two rods to touch a part of their real body and, simultaneously, the same part of their illusory body behind them, they confirmed sitting behind their actual body and noticing their real body from there.

In the second study, dying people where weighted and, after their vital signs stopped, it was observed that their actual weight decreased. This experiment was conducted by Dr Duncan MacDougall in Massachusetts, and his results were published in prestigious medical journals and the New York Times. Apparently, the mass lost in four of the six studied cases was about 21 grams, and ever since, the hypothesis has been widely circulated that this weight corresponds to the weight of the soul. When the physician repeated the experiment with fifteen dogs, no change in the body mass values had been noticed, and he concluded that only humans possess souls.

Many informative surveys have also been created online by researchers of this phenomenon, and the results were extracted from thousands of responses. Most of the internet users that took part in the surveys have declared that they have felt, at least once, one of the common sensations associated with out-of-body experiences. Jolts, sudden low or high frequency sounds, or bodily vibrations are only a few of them.

Chapter 2 - What Exactly Is Astral Projection?

Defining a phenomenon, whose factual existence is based on testimonials, and relevant, but scarce, empirical evidence is open to interpretations. Basically, astral projection is an out-of-body experience that engages the sensorial system and whose effects are mostly of a psychological nature. The platform on which it relies is not necessarily related to beliefs or desires, but is dependent on sensitive self-awareness. However, its long-term usage and the mostly positive consequences resulting from such incidents support its high relatedness among humans.

Astral projection, regardless of the causes and intentions associated with it, voluntarily or involuntarily, is an experience that fascinates and stimulates our minds and imaginations, as it is an outstanding route one can follow to personal enlightenment. It represents feasible proof that the significance of our lives could rise above terrestrial limitations. It's also a manner to confront and defeat the fears of uncertain circumstances, and the unknown, that so many times extends beyond our control.

In the following paragraphs, you will discover the most important interpretations, whose validity cannot be contested in relation to astral projection.

Supernatural Affair

Beyond religious, cultural, and spiritual interpretations, astral projection is a supernatural manifestation in which one's astral body separates from the physical one, and travels through higher or lower dimensions, or around the physical world.

It is assumed that the fifth dimension is the one usually chosen, the extra dimension that is the subject of many astrophysics and mathematics preoccupations. We live in a 4-dimension world, three spatial and one time dimension. Hypothetically, the concept of a fifth dimension could mean an alternative world in which one could make different life choices and travel into.

The astral plane of existence can be inhabited by various entities or can be unpopulated. The journey can be made in different times and spaces, and during its unfolding, the astral body's connection with the physical body is not ceased and cannot be broken. A silver cord or astral cord maintains, at all times, the bond between the two.

Because other astral bodies can coexist in the same astral plane, the encounters with them are considered very probable. Furthermore, if the astral plane is composed of spheres associated with hells, heavens, and other ethereal spaces occupied by beings such as angels, demons, or specters, it is possible to interact and communicate with them too. Hence, astral projection can prove to be not only an individual, but also a social affair.

Art of Transcendent Liberation

Astral projection is the proper art of detaching one's consciousness from their material self and transferring it to the spiritual one. Then, through discipline and concentration, the astral body is capable of leaving its shelter, the mortal form, and traveling away from it. Its liberation is meant to enrich and release, through transcendent elevation and cognition, its possessor. It's the pursuance of that feeling, materialized in random thoughts, such as "I just wish I could fly away from everything and release myself of my worries! Just be totally free!", which we all can relate to at some point in time.

Even though it is teachable and malleable, astral projection can occur during sleep time too. That is because the astral body can follow the subconscious wishes of the person to whom it belongs. So, at times, if the intensity of one's desire is powerful enough, through the realm of dreaming, one can perceive an out-of-body experience too. In this case, it is meant as an act of fulfillment of real aims that otherwise might not be accessible or unperceived.

"Last Act" Anticipation

Intimately associated with reincarnation and afterlife, astral projection can be employed as a valuable instrument in studying the dying process. No, it is not meant to enhance the gloominess one might feel when thinking about the last act our corporeal bodies undergo in the earthly world. It is an anticipative model, whose purpose is to help you comprehend this natural, inevitable process, and even to embrace it when your time finally comes. In fact, it can easily be viewed as a sort of simulation of the finale. The only major difference is that when the physiological demise occurs, the astral body's connection with the physical body is severed.

Near death experiences stand as solid attestations for the reliability astral projection possesses when it comes to researching the physical death. Most of the people who have come across such crucial events have reported going through out-of-body episodes, and clearly seeing the image of the physical figure left behind. The essential fact to retain from these accounts is that, after living through these incidents, and getting back into their bodies, these people have lost all their fears related to death. The euphoric state they reached during their near death experiences, through floating and flying in spiritual form away from their bodily form, is the same that people Describe who willingly practice astral projection.

Lastly, an important fact to acknowledge is that, even though it can be felt in various ways by different people, astral projection is essentially the same phenomenon. Whether it's discerned as religious illumination, personal insight, or a path to salvation from mortal anxieties and pressures, astral projection is an extraordinary manner to progress on all levels of your existence, and evolve your individuality.

Chapter 3 - How Does It Happen?

So, now that you know what astral projection means, how it can be used, and in what particular situations it can be triggered, it is time for you to find out how it works. How does it happen? How can one differentiate it from a vision generated by a wish for it to happen, or from a dream in which it appeared to have happened? Well, accidental or intentional, this phenomenon is naturally designed in steps, that, with small variations from a person to another, indicate its passage.

1. Pre-Astral Projection Indicators

Before the astral journey begins, a series of symptoms of physical and psychological nature, announce that the experience is about to happen. These signs constitute a preparation process for your body and mind, so as to make possible the spiritual projection. Your focus shifts from surroundings to inner perceptions and your self-awareness is awakened.

Sensorial Signs - When one prepares for, or spontaneously is close to experiment an astral travel, they will often *hear sudden sounds* of various intensities, such as humming, buzzing, or howling. It is also possible to perceive actual voices or other sounds such as of objects falling. However, the buzzing noise is the most commonly signaled, and, in some cases, can rise to barely tolerable levels.

Another sensation that can and does happen in anticipation of the astral projection is *optical hallucinations*. Before your physical body enters the specific trance state for the astral body to undergo its journey, you can see things. These can range from mixtures of colors and patterns of shapes to fantastic scenes and visions. Some people can see a tunnel and a light at its end, a common depiction in near-death experiences.

Catalepsy, sleep paralysis, or bodily rigidity, is also a common pre-indicator of astral travel. The feeling that your body can't move is many times associated with the inability to speak. It can be scary, but this is often assimilated with a dream-like state and in fact, if no fear shadows it, it relaxes the body.

Modifications such as *irregular or fast heartbeats* can also be experienced. It might be due to a rush of emotion, such as uneasiness or elation, or an initiatory requirement. A clear explanation doesn't exist, but it doesn't seem to influence the subsequent voyage negatively.

Shortness of breath can be felt too, but, just as the increased heart rate, it's a symptom that usually subsides as soon as you proceed with the astral projection.

Psychosomatic Signs - Besides physical changes that indicate the development of an out-of-body experience, significant psychological happenings add to the body's preparation for its spiritual travel component.

The most familiar sign in this category is related to movements. Not physical movements, but movements that are internally perceived. Specifically defined as *vibrations,* these progressive little waves, felt throughout your body, without actually any physical response, are believed to represent the most defining symptom of astral projection.

Another psychosomatic sign that supports the suggestion of further astral travel is *dizziness.* A sensation of falling, flying, or being suspended typically dominate in this case. It directly implies that your astral body is ready to be released from its bodily confinement.

A *weight shift* feeling can accompany the emotional manifestations that precede your astral projection. You can suddenly become aware of the fact that your body feels heavy or very light, as if your bodily mass has dropped or has suddenly risen.

Bodily temperature fluctuation can as well be discerned. A coldness sensation or, on the contrary, a heat flush can come over you.

2. The Actual Process

When the astral body detaches from the physical body, one is clearly aware of it. Unlike the case when you dream or self-induce a state of vision, you often notice your bodily self laying on the bed after you rise above it, and sometimes the cord that connects you to it is visible too. Also, the surrounding details keep their integrity. Unlike in a dream or vision, where alterations to the material world happen, during the actual astral journey, everything related to the physical world you are traveling in and across, is unchanged. You won't find yourself in a strange place all of a sudden, but will travel there from your detachment moment. This is a fundamental element that distinguishes astral projection from sought after visualizations and dreams.

The astral body is not affected by gravity and its ethereal manifestation is not governed by other physical laws. So, it can fly, float, or fall. Also, even though it can travel through the material world, your spiritual form isn't capable of touching objects or beings or feeling them. So, it will go through them. Yes, that means passing through walls and people. However, when it comes to objects and creatures that inhabit the astral plane, the astral body can feel, touch, and acknowledge them, just as the earthly body does in the physical world. So, your thinking processes and senses do not get lost, but they get applied to another level.

Because there are no actual rules or limits in the astral dimensions, it is mostly what you make of it. Your mind models it, and your feelings determine most of the experiences that occur in the astral plane. Notions as up, down, left, and right are perceived only because your mindset is contouring them, based on your physical existence. Furthermore, your vision is in fact, an all-encompassing 360 degrees view. Also, there are distinct energetic levels that you can reach on the astral plane dependent on your thoughts and intentions. The entities you come into contact with usually inhabit different levels based on their similarities too.

3. *Post-Astral Projection Indicators*

Just as there are certain triggering symptoms that lead to astral projection, there also are specific signs that occur at the end of this spiritual journey. These signs, as they mark the end of an astral journey, have a psychological impact, and seldom manifest physiologically.

Vivid *recollections* from the travel usually indicate its occurrence. It can be argued that these can be the results of an imaginative process, but when astral projecting during a wakeful state is engaged, even though not tangible, these can illustrate loyal representations from the material world, and also from the astral plane.

A pervading sense of total *calmness* has been noticed often in people that went through out-of-body experiences. Whether this is a side effect, prompted by the consequent grasp of one's boundless spiritual existence, or a direct impact caused by the temporary release of the spiritual self, its presence has been widely affirmed.

Some people apparently develop *healing and foretelling* abilities, through learning to channel their inner energies in positive astral projections. It is generally assumed that unleashing one's awareness in higher dimensions can allow one to overrule the limitations enforced on their overall being by the physical existence.

Chapter 4 – How Can You Travel the Astral Plane?

As it has been previously mentioned, some people get to travel spiritually without any intention, while finding themselves in critical situations, induced by circumstances such as near-death experiences and dreams. Meanwhile, other people do it intentionally, whether by means of intense practice (meditation, self-discipline), or using additional help (hypnosis, hallucinogenic drugs, research studies). This guide is elaborated to provide you the exact information on how to prepare and travel the astral plane through self-thought practice.

Possible enhancers, which are helpful and harmless instruments that can help you facilitate the astral projection, will be indicated here too. However, you must keep in mind that the most important tool in order to succeed is your will. As long as you truly desire to experiment with this phenomenon, and have decided to channel your energy towards achieving this goal, no substantial impediment can stop you from doing so. The only barriers are the ones your own mind creates, but you will also be advised here about how you can release yourself from anxieties and doubts and strengthen your motivation.

Step by step, you will now learn how to safely adventure on an astral journey in realms that you have only imagined or dreamed about. Firstly, you need to get yourself ready physically and mentally, then try the most popular techniques described below, and, based on the outcome, select the one that suits you best. Because our personalities differ, and we possess distinct levels of awareness and imaginative capability, the only way to figure out the most effective method for you is to test the few renowned ones presented here. Lastly, you need to stick with the one you feel most comfortable with, and develop your astral travel skills from there.

Physical Preparation

It is very important for the setting in which your out-of-body experience happens to be safe, convenient, and relaxed, so that no worldly disturbances will occur and affect the success of your spiritual projection.

Surroundings - Usually, the most recommended location would be your bedroom, the *place* where you should feel most protected and at peace with yourself. But if you don't live alone, and you share your most intimate space with someone else, it is not a good idea, as it can easily get you distracted. So, in this case, the thing to do is choose another room. Whether it is in your own home or somewhere else, it is crucial for this place to be safe.

It is ideal that your location is not in the middle of a busy area, or nearby a rail station or airport, as noises can make it hard for you to ignore the background and focus on your internal processes. However, if these can't be avoided, use soft earplugs or earphones. Yes, it will further be explained how music can be incorporated in your mental preparation for the astral travel.

Close the windows, lock the door, and check that devices such as mobile or home phone, TV, and others are turned off. Also, make sure no one will actually come around during this time, invited or not. You wouldn't want to be interrupted at the exact moment when you are about to take off into the astral plane, would you?

The best *time* of the day to practice astral projecting is very early in the morning. Some people do it during the night too, but it is more likely that your mind is lucid and capable of focusing after a good night's rest. This time frame is also desirable, because human activity is almost nonexistent before dawn, so the peacefulness around you can only assist your spiritual endeavor.

Another important element of your surroundings is the *temperature*. It depends on the season, but you should regulate the heating or the air conditioning so as to create a slightly warm atmosphere. This is because your bodily temperature often drops while your astral body travels away from your material body.

Body - When it comes to *clothing*, opt for loose and soft attire. Your casual pajamas will do. Otherwise, you can also wear nothing at all, but in that situation, you should cover your body with a light blanket or sheet, as it could get cold while its astral double travels away.

A very common *position* of one's physical body, when getting ready for a voluntary out-of-body experience, is lying on the bed on your back, while keeping the limbs stretched, forming a continual line. Your eyes should be closed so they will not be attracted to details in your vicinity.

The next thing to do is *relax your muscles*. Loosen whatever tension might be in them, and become aware of all your parts, from head to toe. Gradually advance from forehead to your neck, chest, back, and tummy, while going through each limb. Move slowly, and then fully relax.

The *breathing* should be deep and slow. Inhale and exhale without rush, and release the stiffness that might be accumulated in your chest and shoulders. Embrace a sluggish, yet steady pattern.

Mental Preparation

When your body is fully relaxed and has reached a similar state as the one preceding sleep, you must prepare your mind accordingly to stay focused and alert. That is because when you are astral projecting, your body enters a sleep mode, the difference being that your mind doesn't accompany it, but remains awake. Simply, what you must obtain in order to astral travel is a modified condition of awareness. The mental consciousness is active and accompanying your astral body, while your physical body remains in an inactive state, as when sleeping.

Relaxation - Our mind wanders all the time, and the most pregnant thoughts are the ones related to worries, problems to solve, things to do, targets to achieve, and so on. It is a scientifically proven fact that many of us tend to fret over the most insignificant details and events that are part of our earthly existence. So, how does one relax while keeping their body still? How can this be done in order to further allow particular focus on a transcendent phenomenon? Well, read further and you will find out the responses to these questions.

Music - Different music genres have sounds emitted at various frequencies, and their effect on the brainwaves is consequently varied. Isochronic tones, along with monaural and binaural tones, have been studied and concluded to represent stimuli that determine a frequency change inside the human brain, which leads to hemispheric synchronization. This condition is apparently correlated with health benefits such as high concentration, control over pain, and stress management. It is the reason why people that meditate or practice astral projection listen to relaxation music with these beats.

Essential Oils - It has been remarked that certain essential oils have the capacity to enhance psychic experiences. Whether applied directly on your skin, in certain areas such as forehead, wrists, the back of the neck, and ankles, or kept in a diffuser that spreads their scent, these plant extracts can help you relax completely. Most frequently, frankincense, cinnamon, jasmine, myrrh, and rosemary derived oils are the ones selected.

Herbs - Prepared as teas and consumed before comfortably positioning your body on the bed for the subsequent astral projection, or stuffed in small sacks that release their scent, many herbs with protective, healing, and relaxing effects can be reliable additional helpers.

Probably the most popular herb utilized to ease astral projection is moonwort, widely employed for prophecies and guardianship during the ancient times. Associated with witchcraft and apparently omnipresent in flying ointments, its genus name, "Artemisia", derives from the Greek goddess of the moon, Artemis. Other herbs include honeysuckle, valerian, bay, wintergreen, chamomile, and eyebright.

Crystals - Certain gemstones have also been deployed for travel in the astral plane, as some have calming and stress releasing properties. Fear, anxiety, and irritability of all sorts can be kept at bay or simply cast away with the help of crystals such as prehnite, aventurine, blue calcite, lithium quartz, sugilite, and magnesite.

Concentration - After removing all the potential mental obstacles through relaxation, it is necessary to channel the mind in the particular direction it needs to enter into astral projection. Focus is a key factor preceding the practical access into astral realms through spiritual detachment. As long as your motivation is solid and you thoroughly relaxed your mind and body, there is no actual reason that could prevent you from centralizing your awareness on a single track.

Autosuggestion - The easiest way to gather your streams of consciousness into a uniform flux, and to center your thinking on the out-of-body-experience you are about to live, is by means of autosuggestion. Engage your inner voice and direct your thoughts towards positive self-assurance. Repeat as if they were religious prayers or a magical rite's brief sentences, such as "I am going to do it, I will travel in the astral plane", "I will succeed with my astral projection", or "I am gifted and I will ascertain my out-of-body experience".

It might seem a bit silly or futile at first, but remember what you read before. Your will and state of mind dictate your actual capability. Don't let doubts and impatience take a hold on you. Saying and repeating, while strongly believing, extends your self-awareness and eventually leads to achievement.

Imaginative self-observation - Mostly a meditative exercise, this focus challenge engages your creative power. Remember that astral projection, just as any other significant pursuit, is an art. To discover new worlds, it is important to discern their nuances, shapes, and textures. In this case, your mind is the canvas on which you paint, so you learn to distinguish clearly. The more you use it, the more likely you are to create the essential mental gate through which you can release your spiritual form. But no, there is no need to actually imagine the new world.

Instead, here is what you have to do. With your eyes closed, and your body relaxed as much as possible, you imagine a part of your body that is moving. You meditate over this image until it feels as vivid as a real one. Physically, you don't move, let's say your arm or foot, but mentally, you create a powerful image of it moving. Then, you channel your energy in it. By means of power, will, and imagination, you collect all the vital energy scattered inside your body and concentrate it in your limb. From that site, you can engage one of the techniques succinctly presented in the following paragraphs to liberate your spiritual being.

Top 10 Easiest and Most Effective Astral Travel Techniques

Many techniques of astral projection have been developed across history, but the suitability of each of them for one individual or another cannot be guaranteed. However, there are a few effective methods that most people have recorded success with, and those are described below for you to select from, according to your needs and skills. Of course, in order to establish the right one for you, you must attempt them all, but that shouldn't constitute a problem, as the whole process doesn't usually require more than a few minutes, ten at most. However, you shouldn't devote a single day to try them all. Use them gradually, one at a time.

1. The Visualization Technique

This meditation method is probably the easiest way to astral projection. It is mainly a matter of directed focus, and it engages your mind's power to visualize. Just as when concentrating, you visualize something real. It could be your own body, another person, an object situated in your close proximity, or a location where you intend to astral travel. All other unrelated thoughts must be ignored and pushed aside.

If you visualize your *physical body*, then you must create its corresponding spiritual double. Then slowly, you begin to move it part by part above your real figure, and progressively involve your whole astral body. Your purpose is to visualize the transfer of your physical perceptions to your spiritual form. The next thing to do is float. Yes, you imagine seeing your astral body floating above your physical one. Your sense of physical awareness will gradually attenuate until the vibrations will take over. Regardless, you keep your focus on imagining your spiritual body hovering above, and watching your physical body from there. Eventually, as the vibratory state intensifies, your astral shape is released and you can see your relaxed, real body in a state of relaxed sleep beneath you, and the silver cord attaching you to it.

If you visualize *another person or an object* present in your room, you should be aware of their precise location. Then, you literally set your mind on reaching the other person or the object. In your astral form, you exit from the physical body and project yourself in the material world at first. From there, you can adventure in the astral plane only by thinking of it.

If you visualize *an actual place,* whether you've traveled there before or not, you must have at least a photograph that you can study. Memorize the landscape and, after relaxation, picture yourself exiting your body and flying inside the actual place. Preceded by the overall vibrations, your astral body will liberate itself and reach for the place. And so, your explorations begin.

2. The Mirror Technique

This method can be a great way to improve your visualization skills. It involves a real mirror, one in which you can see your whole body, that must be placed where it allows you to see your full reflection. Observe every detail of your body clearly, from head to toe, while taking in the surroundings too. Notice its shape, its position, and practice little movements. Your centre of attention is your reflection. Examine it as if it's a painting or drawing you must reproduce.

After a while, close your eyes, but keep the image still. Focus on the way your body is reflected in the mirror, its exact outline, the lights or shadows on it. Begin to move your reflection's body as your own body moves: your fingers, your eyes, your arms and legs. Keep your body relaxed until it reaches a state of sleep, while you visualize your reflection.

Then, imagine rising from your bed and walking around the room. Feel the bare floor or the soft, warm carpet beneath your feet. Pay attention to all the sensations associated with your movement. Your breathing, the objects you see, the contraction, and relaxation, of your moving muscles. As you do so, the transfer of awareness from your sleepy body to your astral one, the mirror's reflection, will occur. You will then perceive new details around you and things that you haven't noticed or paid attention to before. The color or fabric of an item, the positioning of a piece of furniture compared to another, etc. Maintain your calmness and enjoy the new sensations.

3. The Rope Technique

Originally developed by Robert Bruce, a famous astral projection practitioner, this technique is mostly based on tactile sensations. So, if you don't have a well-developed visual memory, but your imagination is not a problem when it comes to sensory feelings, this might be the one for you.

The central object in this case is a rope - an imaginary one that you must mentally project as hanging from the ceiling. Using the imaginary hands of your astral form, you reach towards it and then pull yourself up on it. Hand over hand, you advance with your climbing, and a feeling of vertigo will now begin to build up in your body. Do not stop. Keep focusing on the strong rope, whose texture and width you can sense, and on your ascension. As you do so, you will soon feel vibratory waves going through your body. Continue to climb. Further, you will perceive your astral body coming out of your physical body and reaching for the rope. Next, released of it, it will float above, around the ceiling. And your astral journey now begins.

4. The Ladder Technique

Practically, this technique is very similar to the previous one, but in this case you will use a ladder. This is more indicated if you don't feel you could handle such a task in real life, or that you couldn't rely exclusively on your upper body parts to climb up something. So, a ladder that ends near the ceiling is the object you aspire to climb on until you reach its top.

Using your feet and hands too, you follow the same steps described in the rope technique until you manage to finally liberate your astral body.

5. The Swing Technique

Just as the name suggests, this technique involves another object, a swing. For this method, as for the ladder and rope ones, you can actually experience the real sensations by real life attempts. This way, the feelings of the actual motion will be easier to recall and build up with your imagination.

Completely relaxed, and in a state of deep concentration, just as before, you imagine a swing on which you sit. Be aware of the way your hands grasp the swing's ropes, acknowledge the way your feet dangle in the air beneath you. As you begin your movement, focus on the air that gently brushes your face and moves through your hair. Move faster and feel the air's pressure against your chest, the whizzing in your ears, and the slight tension in your shoulders. While swinging higher and higher, you will perceive signs signaling the further projection. Unusual sounds, electric vibration, shortness of breath. As these occur, picture yourself suddenly falling or flying up from the moving swing. It is the moment when your exit happens.

Detach your astral body from your physical one, and proceed to traveling where you initially intended to.

6. The Tunnel Technique

This method involves an image whose popularity is widespread in accounts of involuntary out-of-body experiences such as near death experiences. The vision's central element is not the tunnel itself, but the light at the end of it. As you probably anticipate, the light is what you endeavor to reach.

Draw a mental picture of a tunnel, and then visualize yourself entering it. At the beginning, you will be surrounded by complete darkness, but little by little, its presence will feel reassuring. Move through it step by step, aiming for its end, the light, which might seem like a faraway point. As you intensify the light's sparkle and its dimension, also increase your pace. If you started walking, progress to running. Run fast as if you were in a race, and at the end, imagine yourself flying or floating into the light. Usually, the actual separation will be assisted by its precursory symptoms and will materialize when you leave the tunnel.

7. The Fall Technique

The free falling technique is in fact very simple. Unrelated to surroundings or external representations, this one is exclusively focused on your actual body, just like the visualization one.

While lying comfortably and relaxed on your bed, and almost reaching the near the trance state, try to become aware of the solid mattress beneath you. Feel the way your body is pressed against its even surface.

Then, focus your mind on causing a falling sensation. Envisage your body falling through the bed, through the floor, even through the earth. At first, do it slowly: your palms sinking down a little, then your heels. Continue until half of your horizontal body is below the line of the bed sheet. The weight of the body becomes less and less material, as if made of an ethereal matter. Then, sink further, increasing the speed of your falling. Do it until your astral body falls out of your actual body, hitting the ground, or the specific symptoms of projections take over. In the latter case, continue until you stop falling and find yourself defying gravity, flying, or floating above your actual body, still and asleep on the bed.

8. The Jump Technique

Similar to the free falling and visualization techniques, the jump method also involves your body and inducing an image of its moving. It is based on the fact that, while the real body obeys gravity and other laws of physics, the astral one isn't restricted by material limits. In real life, when you jump, you end up landing on the ground. When you astral travel, you fly, rotate, or float into the air, as the material ground is not necessary to support your immaterial mass.

The first step is to simply jump while awake. You will obviously hit the ground. Continue to do so during the day as to convince yourself that you are moving in the real world.

Then, early in the morning or after a nap, when you're relaxed and rested, you can decide to astral project. Let yourself reach the needed sleepy state. What's more, allow yourself to fall asleep this time. While your awareness, of course, is maintained alert. Remember, a real out-of-body experience through astral projection is a conscious choice that involves an awake mind and a mostly asleep body.

As you enter the dreams realm, with your consciousness still in an active state, make yourself jump, just as you did during the day in real life. This time, you won't hit the ground. So, through your lucid dreaming, you get out of your body and astral project. Your proof is your conscious jump. Begin to explore the fantastic realm in which you find yourself.

9. The Roll out Technique

When we sleep, we tend to roll over to one side or the other. Whether to reach a more comfortable position, or while dreaming, we often find ourselves in different postures when waking up. The roll out technique is based specifically on that.

Engaging your will and imagination, you project your astral body rolling to the right or the left. Make sure you do keep your physical body still and relaxed as required. As you focus on the rolling movement that your spiritual double undertakes, you will soon reach a dizziness state, and the typical vibrations will emerge. The separation will finally occur, and your astral form will roll out of your corporeal form.

10. The Muldoon's Thirst Technique

Practitioner and author in the field of astral projection, Sylvan Muldoon, developed this technique, taking in consideration one of most intense physical demands, thirst. This method entails a factual state of your real body: deprivation of water.

For a couple of hours before attempting astral travel, do not consume fluids at all. Then, a bit before beginning the process, place a glass or bottle of water in the vicinity of the place where the actual phenomenon will occur. It is even recommended to eat a bit of salt, or a food with high salt content to amplify your craving for drinking water.

After going into your relaxation state, concentrate your attention on your thirst and picture yourself getting up, walking to the nearby source of alleviation, and lifting it up. Step by step, repeat these processes until you reach the dreamy state. Then, as the specific signs take over your actual body, the astral one will eventually liberate itself and reach for the bottle or glass of water.

In a modified version, where no actual source of water is utilized, your astral body might lead you to another source of water from the real world.

How Long Does It Take?

Astral projecting is a spiritual occurrence that each and every one of us can experience, but the time required for a successful travel differs individually. For some it takes weeks, for others months, while there are people that effectively travel on their first attempt. The crucial thing is that you must not get discouraged or feel desolate over it, you need to persist and strengthen your belief in the process. Often, the unconscious doubts and fears are the ones that obstruct us from connecting with our spiritual double, and validate its presence by its liberation from the material form. However, by means of constant practice and deep commitment, the access will be made in time.

When it does happen, note the amount of time spent outside your physical body. As you become more familiar and skilled in astral travel, your capability to control the phenomenon and the necessary time for it will significantly grow. If at the beginning you find yourself spending seconds in the astral realm, you can go as far as tens of minutes. Take into consideration that the notions of time and space are applicable only in the real world, so a few seconds in the physical world might feel like days or weeks in the astral plane.

Chapter 5 - Understanding the Benefits of Astral Projection

The benefits of astral projection extend beyond our material existence. You might decide to attempt traveling in the astral plane out of a sense of curiosity, religiosity, or eagerness for a supernatural experience. Or you might in fact want to find some answers about yourself, or something that happened or happens to you. Whatever your reason might be, you will receive much more than you hoped for. Because the profound modification that astral projection can cause in your being, influences not only your mental and emotional perceptions of life, death, and meaning, but your physical world as well. Below, you will find the 10 most important and precious rewards you will gain in your spiritual journey.

1. Metaphysical Awakening

Living in a universe governed by laws, and self-imposed, or otherwise imposed boundaries can feel a bit frustrating or stifling at times. Making a connection with your astral self, and awakening your divine perceptions, shatters all the limits that restrict you in the material world. If you are a faithful person, this will directly affect your spirituality, and facilitate a direct bond with your adored one(s). If, on the contrary, your belief vibrates in the energy flow scattered within your being, you will reach the deepest levels of self-awareness and the most intimate knowledge about your being's meaning. This effect depends on your personal ideology, but its ultimate contribution is the same: producing the unswerving liberation of your metaphysical consciousness.

2. Enhanced Imagination

Because it continually provokes your ordinary views and your creative potential, by means of visualization, detailed examination and concentration on natural or fantastic elements, astral travel augments your imagination. The more you practice it, the more you will be inclined to break free from the common paths and patterns of thinking, and the immediate result will be seen in your productivity. Imagination is what we engage to evolve beyond our bodily confinement, but it's also the essential tool for finding real life solutions for various types of problems. So this considerable advantage will greatly reflect in your real life choices too, and it can only lead to positive and prosperous outcomes.

3. Extrasensory Abilities

Properties such as healing, telepathy, and foretelling are usually characteristics in legends, fairytales, and intensely debated accounts. The truth is, all of them are attainable. Through astral projection, as you align and unite your constituent parts, the astral and physical bodies, you remove all the emotional blockages that impeded you before from grasping your surroundings beyond mundane intuition. As you become skilled in traveling in higher energetic levels, and the frequencies on which you emit and receive signals from the bodies around you advance, it is possible to communicate with other beings at mystic levels. Whether they reside in the material or spiritual realm, you can bond with them, and influence their health state and yours, be it corporeal or emotional.

4. Liberation of Death Fears

How many times have you looked up into the sky and wished you were a bird, free of your gravity obeying bodily mass, able to fly up high? And how many times did you tremble within, at the thought of your inevitable ending on this earth? You've surely wondered about death and dreaded its apparently decisive power. When you fly into spiritual worlds you only dreamed about, you not only fulfill a dream of unrestrained-to-ground liberty, but you also release yourself from the fears of the finale. Because you discover that it's really nothing to fear, but rather to embrace. It's a weightless flight, an unbounded journey, during which regrets of lost time and longings for faraway spaces never occur. As time and space and outer laws don't exist anymore, the only barriers are the ones your spirits sets.

5. Life after Death Confirmation

An out-of-body experience doesn't just disclose that there is nothing to fear about the final detachment of your spiritual body from your physical one, but also reveals death is the final stop for your worldly shape. It's basically an astral projection that isn't followed by returning to your material form, as the silver cord that kept you tied to it has broken. Your very essence, the soul, lives on, and, if desired, it can actually return in another suitable earthly figure. Or it can fly up into your personal heaven and live happily there for an eternity.

6. Personal Growth

Most of the people that went through near-death experiences, or other similar involuntary out-of-body incidents, declared how their perspective on living and its quality changed. Traveling in the astral plane not only consolidates your self-assurance and incites unsuspected powers and abilities, but it also elevates you. If our personal development was a pyramid, the ideal state would be reached at the top. How many people expect to actually touch their highest aspirations? And how many actually do? It is easy to respond to these questions if you consider that most of them never progress beyond earth-bound circumstances. But when one dwells and ponders beyond that, the respect for life in its complete unfolding will sharpen. And so will the empathy and the love for self and others, which is what helps guide your steps to the highest level of the pyramid.

7. Time Travel

Remember, time and space are material representations, and valid only for a universe whose mass can be evaluated. Since in the astral plane, time doesn't exist, you can move in whatever dimension you wish. So, going back or forth, moving between past and future, while your physical body is caught in the present is not an unrealistic objective anymore. From ancient times to the Renaissance, and from there all the way to current times and a futuristic after time, you can visit them all. Obviously, this will not happen on your first attempt at astral projection, because your skills must be suitably developed. Still, this is possible.

8. Retrospective Comprehension

By traveling in time and space, even getting to meet yourself while in previous lives, you can obtain explanations for the way you are, who you are, and what your actual purpose is for your actual existence. Or you can simply find out something from the not faraway past, something that perhaps occurred in your childhood, and you want to explore and understand it. Whatever your aim, through astral projection, you can better realize a meaning, or a fact that previously might have seemed senseless, distressing, or too dull.

9. Tonic Relaxation

As you get in tune with yourself, and practically solve the mysterious puzzle of your own biography, you will gradually achieve an unparalleled state of relaxation. No disturbance will affect you as it used to before, and no obstacle will ever afflict you that much to make you feel defenseless and defeated. A peaceful sentiment will accompany you wherever you go, as long as you maintain a smooth communication with your spiritual self, and banish all the passing and damaging concerns.

10. Complete Self-Coordination

Because your energy flow is uninterrupted and your every pore, whether physical or spiritual, is coordinated with the surrounding ones, your inner organization will be impeccable. And it will reflect in your outer one accordingly. Discipline and orderly arrangement are key factors for achieving success and fulfilling aspirations, as perseverance is usually associated with them. Through astral projection, you will acknowledge exactly what you are looking for, the means to obtain it, and you will structure your endeavors to satisfy your inner and outer purposes.

Chapter 6 - Can Astral Projection Be Dangerous?

There are many people out there expressing fears about the potential dangers astral projection might bring about, but most of their fears are related to personal anxieties, and not proven occurrences. However, it is normal to fret over something you are not familiar with, especially when it involves an intense involvement in the process. Moreover, even though it is similar for most people, individually it can manifest differently. The 5 most common fears related to astral travel, and their necessary clarifications, are addressed in the following paragraphs.

1. Can One Be Possessed During Astral Projection?

Entities of all types reside in the astral realm, some of them malicious, others angelic. The first ones' energy is low, the latter's is high. It is believed that vibrating at very low energetic levels can allow demonic beings to attempt to possess one's physical body when they are away astral traveling. However, in order for them to do so, most of the time, you will have to invite them to. If you don't, and you don't seek to astral travel to mainly escape your physical body, but to explore your astral one, there is no reason to fear. A strong connection with your body will not permit any other being to enter it. It is perfectly built for you only.

2. Is It Possible To Die While Astral Traveling?

The silver cord that ties your astral and physical body can not normally be severed, broken, or stretched to the point of breaking. Normally, no foreign astral body can cut it. On the other hand, your physical body is vulnerable while you astral travel, in the sense that it can be harmed in ways that could happen during sleep. That's why it is of uttermost importance to astral project in a very safe place.

3. Will You Always Return Safely To Your Physical Body?

Your physical body is the home of your astral body, so you will never forget the way back to it. In fact, this is only a matter of will. In an instant, if you imagine it, you can return to your body from wherever you might have projected yourself.

4. Can You Get Blocked In The Astral Plane?

No, unless you let yourself be overwhelmed by fears of getting lost or blocked. Your mental state is in charge of the things that happen to you. So, if you remain strong and confident at all times, there is no reason to believe that you will get stuck outside your body.

5. Does Your Physical Body Get Exhausted Because Of It?

At the end of an astral projection, your body will actually feel as refreshed and rested as after a good night's sleep. Only your spirit is engaged in the astral voyage.

Conclusion

I hope this book was able to help you understand what astral projection is, and how easy it is to achieve it, even though many people still see it as an unreachable utopia. You should now be able to distinguish between involuntary incidents, such as dreaming, and near death experiences occurring in unconscious states, and astral travel, an out-of-body experience undergone in a conscious state.

Practiced for various reasons throughout history, and widely debated, derided, or aspired to, astral projection is an excellent and unique path to follow in order to deepen your self-awareness, solidify your religious devotion, and shed away all your anxieties. It's the actual proof that our significance extends beyond our mortal lives, and that the feared grand finale is only a permanent spiritual liberation.

By following the specific steps described in this guide, you will surely manage to personally evolve and enhance your psychic, mental, and emotional capacities so as to improve the quality of your life. I wish to accentuate again that astral projection is not an appropriate choice for people with psychological disorders. Other than that, if you have prepared accordingly, no issues should occur, if you take into consideration all its subsequent effects and potential risks.

The next step is to try it for yourself, and live all the enriching benefits arriving from it. All it takes is belief, commitment, and perseverance. As with any meaningful endeavor, astral projection must be carefully planned, studied, and prepared for mentally and physically. Only by means of total dedication, and loyal repetition, our effectiveness can improve and our potential can widen. After all, it is what it takes to attain valuable successes and experiences, of whatever type.

Finally, if you enjoyed this book, then I'd like to ask you for a favor, would you be kind enough to leave a review for this book on Amazon? It'd be greatly appreciated!

Lucid Dreaming
A Guide to Lucid Dreaming, and How to Take Control of Your Dreams

Introduction

This book contains proven steps and strategies on how to achieve lucidity in your dreams and begin to control them.

Lucid dreaming is a controversial topic, but an equally fascinating one. Who among us has not wondered what it would be like to be able to be "awake", somehow, during a dream, to be aware, and be able to control it to their satisfaction? The sensation is unlike any other, and it is definitely an experience that everyone should have at least once in their lifetime.

But how do you go about lucid dreaming? How do you get to dream and to control your awareness and your actions? Well, luckily, this e-book is here to answer all of your questions regarding this subject. Allow the book to serve as your ultimate guide to lucid dreaming. Learn everything, from the very basics, to advanced techniques on dream control. It is surely a process and it takes some time to master, but it is entirely worth it, because the experience is truly unique.

Ever had a dream that you never wanted to end? Or have you ever wished you could just be aware during your dreams, so you could control the events and the people around you, and be able to remember everything afterwards? Now you can. It is entirely possible, and many people do it every single night. Flying, interacting with the deceased, and acting upon urges you wouldn't normally in real life; you can do all of that and more in a lucid dream.

Everything you have ever wanted to try or experience can now be yours as easily as enjoying your sleep. Lucid dreaming is not just for those among us that are metaphysically inclined; anyone can do it, with the right knowledge and the proper training. All you need is to genuinely want it, and be willing to begin the process of becoming initiated in the art of lucid dreaming.

Achieving lucidity in your sleep is definitely a skill, and one you and others like you can master, with a little help. This e-book was written with the purpose of helping people who are curious about lucid dreaming, and want to learn about it and get to experience it. It presents relevant and valuable information, it explains the process, and it features techniques, as well as tips and tricks that will help you in your future endeavors.

Don't wait your whole life, wondering what it must be like to experience a lucid dream. Take control – in the dream realm and in the real one – and become initiated in this fascinating art of sleep. Who says sleeping has to be boring or uneventful? Make your dreaming life as exciting as your waking life, or even more so. Take the plunge and learn how to achieve lucidity, awareness, and rationality during your dreams, and there will be no stopping you.

Chapter 1 – What is Lucid Dreaming? Understanding Lucid Dreaming, the Process, and Format

What is lucid dreaming?

Lucid dreaming refers to the action of immersing yourself in a dream, while being aware that you are dreaming. This is where the term "lucid" comes from, it refers to the mental awareness that you are experiencing during the dream. Frederick van Eeden is the one who came up with it in 1913, and it has been used to describe the process ever since. Lucidity usually occurs as soon as the dreamer realizes that they are dreaming. This happens because of certain details that are unlikely (or even impossible) to happen in the real world. Once the dreamer becomes aware of this, they enter a stage of lucid dreaming.

So, essentially, lucid dreaming begins the moment you have the knowledge that you are, indeed, in a dream. But lucid dreaming can also differ in intensity and level of lucidity. You may simply realize that some events have no place in the real world or that you are dreaming, without having control over your actions or the consequences of your actions. Alternatively, you can also be completely aware and in charge of the events occurring in your dream. You know that you are sleeping in your own bed, dreaming, and outside of any kind of immediate danger, and that you can wake up at whatever point you please, because you have that control; you are the one in charge.

A lucid dream presents itself like an alternate reality. Everything feels supremely real and you can sense everything like you would normally would. It is also much sharper than a normal dream, which often feels like a daze. In fact, at times, it can be hard to distinguish between reality and a lucid dream, which is why lucid dreamers employ reality checks, but this is something I will expand upon later on. For now, you need to know that lucid dreams are entirely safe, natural, and healthy. There is nothing weird, scary, or paranormal about it – it is simply a different, *better* way to experience dreams.

All of your experiences are completely authentic-feeling, which is precisely why so many people are fans of lucid dreams. It is a unique opportunity to try things you've never tried before and probably never will, in real life. Flying, exploring space, and time travel are just a few of the incredible experiences you can have. But the best thing about it is that the possibilities are truly endless. You can do anything you want, however you want it; the sky is the limit. In fact, not even the sky, since people have traveled in space in lucid dreams before.

About lucidity

Even though lucid dreaming has a definition you can check, it is not as cut and dry as people would like it to be. Lucidity requires certain clarity of the mind during your dream, but even if you achieve it, there is no guarantee that you will hold onto it. Once you realize you are dreaming, lucidity can come and go as you continue to be immersed in the dream world. You may be aware that you are in a dream and attempt to control it, by having yourself do something impossible in the real world, only to have the dream take over again, as you once again lose your mental clarity to the sleep process.

Some may think that being lucid during a dream means that you are rational, but that is far from the truth. Even if you are aware of the fact that you are currently in a dream, your brain is still not fully "awake" and functioning at its full capacity, which is why it allows crazy and otherwise silly things to happen during your dream. Our actions are oftentimes ridiculous, stupid, or absurd, and we are not entirely rational; we only *think* we are. The dream world lacks the rules of the real one (either social ones or natural ones), so unusual things are bound to happen, whether we realize it or not.

As previously mentioned, there are various lucidity levels, and each moment of the dream may vary in rationality and understanding. But more often than not, certain irrationality is implied when it comes to dreams, and we are susceptible to doing all sorts of strange things we would not normally be doing. There are certain behaviors that are common, and occur in most subjects while they are lucid dreaming.

One of them is mistakenly believing that people appearing in the dream are real. As in, the dreamer knows that they are in a lucid dream, but they think the people in it are more than a personal projection. This happens because they are often very realistic, clear, or true to real life in behavior. The dreamer is sometimes concerned that the things they do in the dream affect their real-life relationship with the people in it.

Another one is the concern for the thoughts and opinions of others and moral or social consequences. What we are taught in real life, and the way we are socially conditioned is very strong, not only in conscious behavior, but also in an unconscious state. Thus, even though a dreamer may know they are currently in a lucid dream, they will still be worried about getting caught doing things that are normally morally reprehensible, about exposing themselves, or about embarrassing themselves in front of others. If they were to be fully rational, they would realize that there are no such consequences in dreams. Still, irrationality usually wins, and the dreamer may have certain anxieties, reminiscent of real-life social conditioning rules in their dream and its direction.

Similar to social conditioning, the primal fear of danger, and being hurt physically supersedes the momentary awareness of being in a dream. When we are in danger, our instincts take over, and we reflexively enter a fight or flight mode, in which we do whatever it takes to avoid harm. In real life, we can consciously ignore the panicked signals our body sends us to indicate imminent danger (like, say, going on a scary rollercoaster), because we know that there is nothing to *actually* worry about, but in the dream world, we are completely taken over by our senses and reflexes.

Lucid dreaming and dream control

Some people mistakenly equate lucid dreaming and dream control, when that is really not the case. The two are not the same thing, and you can definitely have one without the other. Lucid dreams, over which the dreamer has no control are possible, and so is exercising control over a dream in which they are not entirely lucid. That being said, oftentimes, lucidity grants more control over what happens in the dream, as the dreamer is able to decide what they want to experience.

There is an option for control and to what extent the dreamer wishes to control their dream. This can mean letting events "flow" naturally and seeing where they take them, or the dreamer can decide to create their own personal scenario, bring in other people, etc. Some may believe that at this point, the dreamer is able to do anything, and make anything happen or appear, like in a fictional story. However, that is not always the case. The ability to make things happen relies strongly on the confidence of the dreamer. They need to really believe that they can do something, or else not even the dream world guarantees positive results.

The dangers in lucid dreaming

A common fear that people report is that lucid dreaming might become dangerous in some way, but this fear is largely unfounded. Why? Well, first of all, because most lucid dreams are positive, not negative. And even if a dreamer does find themselves lucid in a nightmare, for example, the awareness that they are, in fact, dreaming, is likely to change the experience for the better. Armed with the knowledge that the dream is not real, the dreamer does not need to be afraid anymore, and instead, they can face their fears or even make them disappear. There is no reason for anyone to be concerned about being lucid in any dream context, nightmare or otherwise, because the experience is most likely to improve, as a result.

Many are afraid of dying in dreams, especially lucid ones, because they fear that they would suffer the same consequence in reality. Not only is that pretty unlikely – impossible, even, unless the dreamer experiences a heart attack, or a similar crisis – it is also difficult to document or keep track of. There are no recorded cases of people dying because of dreams, since there would be no one left to tell us about it, and this is not the type of thing that comes up in an autopsy. People have been dying in dreams since immemorial times, and the experience never had negative consequences in waking life. It can be bizarre, and a little frightening to experience your own death, but just like flying in dreams doesn't translate to real life, neither does dying.

In fact, whatever happens in your dream, even negative events like death, is a projection of your own mind. They are not messages transcending realms, meant to reach you in waking life, but simply models that we, ourselves construct mentally and then act upon. All actions, events, and experiences one has in a dream are dictated, fuelled, and influenced by their fears, hopes, opinions, personal perceptions, motivations, etc. Thus, while dreams cannot predict the future or something similarly enticing, they can act as a means for us to learn more about ourselves, through our unconscious minds' projections.

Lucid dreaming can become addictive, because people come to enjoy the control they are free to exercise in a lucid dream. But far from being a way of life, lucid dreams can help us discover more about ourselves, and the secret motivations that influence our behavior, and can serve as an encouragement to improve our lives.

Can a lucid dream be categorized as an out of body experience?

This is an interesting point that has been long debated – the topic of out of body experiences. Some say that they have had one while engaged in a lucid dream, while others simply claim that a lucid dream facilitates an out of body experience and that they are similar. Several people have described the sensation of physically leaving their bodies and being able to watch it from the "outside".

Lucid dreaming can serve as preparation for an out of body experience, according to people familiar with the experience. People have reported similar sensations for both, so it is not outside the realm of possibility that the two are somehow connected or occur within the same kind of parameters.

Chapter 2 – Why Would You Want to Have Lucid Dreams?

Why do people want to have lucid dreams?

This is a question that is on the mind of a lot of people, especially when they first become familiar with the concept of lucid dreaming. What benefits could lucid dreaming bring someone? Well, if nothing else, lucid dreaming is, without a doubt, one of the most interesting experiences one can have. It is a unique opportunity to experience dreams (that are normally limited and outside of our control) in a new way. The control you can gain over them, and over your actions, and the events happening in them is extraordinarily appealing to a large number of people, and it might be something you find yourself interested in.

People experiment with lucid dreaming for a variety of reasons, from curiosity to others more serious or planned, like healing or stimulating creativity in a new and exciting way. I am going to go into detail for a few of the reasons, as a means of learning more about people's motivations behind the decision to experience lucid dreaming.

Creativity

We already know that our creativity is let loose during the dreaming process, regardless if we are aware or not. That is how we are able to unconsciously create scenarios, characters, and events. It all comes down to unrestricted imagination and brain activity, which is high during REM sleep, and taps into our unconscious mind, with a lack of restrictions normally imposed by waking life and awareness.

This allows our brain to create situations that would be considered strange, to say the least, if not absurd, in real life, but it also stimulates our creativity at the same time. Without the constraints of waking life, our mind is free to imagine, and create whatever is dictated by our fears, desires, hopes, and other hidden or unconscious feelings that only resurface in this way.

These facts are all backed up by scientific research, with various studies showing that our creativity is greatly enhanced by dreaming. Lucid dreaming can lead to more creativity and better problem solving skills.

Transcendence

It is no secret that lucid dreaming can help you connect with your inner self. Through a lucid dream, you can transcend the barriers of consciousness, and relate to your unconscious mind in a way that you are not able to do in any other circumstance. It is a fascinating and unique experience, and it can forever change you and the way you look at yourself and at the world.

You experience the whole world differently, and are aware of different things than in real life. Your senses are altered, and the way you perceive the environment around you, the people you interact with, and your own emotions makes it feel almost like an alternate reality, but one in which you feel everything more intensely.

It may even leave you questioning reality, asking yourself what is real and what is not. As strange as it may sound, it can change your perception forever, and leave you with many questions about yourself, about life, about your existence in this world, and whether it is all a lucid dream. That's why it is often indicated that all people should experience a lucid dream at least once in their lifetime. It can change everything, and it's something you wouldn't want to miss out on.

Fantasy Fulfilment

We spend a lot of our waking hours fantasizing about certain things. Most often, it's sex (or at least, for the males among us), but fantasies come from all sorts of unfulfilled desires. That's why lucid dreams are the ultimate ways to fulfill fantasies that would otherwise remain unexplored. It is a unique opportunity to experience what you have always wanted to, without any kind of consequences, social or otherwise.

You can create infinite pleasure for yourself, in all forms, without the need to feel guilty, or feeling like you've wronged someone in some way. The morality of it can become murky, especially when sexual fantasies are involved, but at the end of the day, it's just a dream, and the exhilaration we feel in dreams is our own, so no one can take that away from us.

Visualizing Success

You know how they say that in waking life, you should always visualize success and being successful, and that in this way, you are going to attain it? Doing so in dreams follows the same idea, only it's much more powerful. Because you're in a lucid dream, the whole experience is much more vivid and intense, and you can practically "taste" your success or fulfilled wish.

This way, you can practice for real-life events like exams, speeches, presentations, or other things where the success relies on your performance. Visualizing your success in any of these situations again and again will help you prepare for the real-life event, and you will seamlessly get through it without a care in the world, because you will feel like you've already done it once or time and time again.

Adventure

Many of us daydream about exciting adventures, but how many really get the opportunity to go on one? Travelling around the world is a goal held by many, but achieved by few. But that doesn't have to be the case for long. Through lucid dreaming, you are able to travel to your heart's content, see parts of the world you've never seen before, or even travel through time. You can be a pirate on a ship, or go to Ancient Egypt, Victorian England, or Colonial America. The world is your oyster and no adventure is out of reach; you are only limited by your own imagination and confidence in your abilities.

Thus, lucid dreaming is the ultimate form of escapism. Sure, books, and movies are great, but nothing compares to feeling everything in first person, as intensely as if it were really happening to you. It's almost like magic, in many ways, so it is the perfect way to take a "vacation" from your normal, boring life, and be a hero with dangerous adventures, once in a while.

Healing

It is a little-known fact, but lucid dreams can, in fact, help one heal from physical wounds or emotional ones. No, dreams don't have magical healing properties, but they can prove invaluable when it comes to pain relief, or working through emotional issues like grief, anxiety, or phobia. This can occur through certain imagery or through empowering actions inside the lucid dream.

It's similar to escapism, in that you look for solutions to your real-life problems in the dream world, or seek to escape the pain of waking life. But it can actually yield impressive results, as far as healing of the mind or of the body goes.

Dealing with Nightmares

There are people in the world who suffer from chronic nightmares or night terrors. It is a horrible thing to live with, when every time you go to sleep, you are anxious about slipping into another nightmare. These conditions can develop because of stress, or because of a traumatic event in the dreamer's life, and are usually solved through therapy.

However, a very effective method is also possible via lucid dreaming. The explanation is simple: with lucid dreams, you are the one in control, as opposed to being controlled by the dream, and you are the one who dictates what happens. It is very empowering, and it can help the affected party regain control over their dreams, and get rid of their nighttime fears.

The simple fact of knowing that they are in charge, and that nothing can hurt them, unless they let it happen is enough to put them at ease, and reduce their anxieties about dreaming. With time, they will learn that their nightmares are only projections of their own fears and repressions, and that they can solve them, work through them, or otherwise eliminate them.

Chapter 3 – How Can You Have Lucid Dreams?

Anyone can have lucid dreams

A common question is whether or not anyone can have lucid dreams. And the answer to that is yes, anyone who wants to can learn how to dream lucidly. With time and practice, any person who wants to have one can learn this valuable skill. All you have to do is inform yourself as best as you can on the matter, and then apply everything you learn. Pay attention to the information presented in this e-book, and you, too, can learn to achieve lucidity, and become an experienced lucid dreamer who can control their dreams effortlessly.

It's true that some people may seem gifted, or have a natural ability for lucid dreaming. It can be an innate skill, but it is usually a developed one. Practice makes perfect, but it is also possible for a person to have a random moment of lucidity while dreaming. However, without being aware of what lucid dreams are, how they work, and how they can prolong their experience, these remain unique happenings. Generally speaking, if you are usually able to remember your dreams in detail, you should not have any great difficulty in achieving lucidity.

Does it take long for someone to have a lucid dream?

As you can imagine, there is no definite answer to this question. It is all a matter of personal inclination, as well as practice, focus, and frequency of meditation. So, basically, there is no set timeframe, and each individual learns at their own pace. As I mentioned earlier, the ability to remember your dreams contributes greatly to your ease of becoming lucid during a dream.

Some people have managed to induce their first lucid dream in only a few days, others in a couple of weeks, with most people reporting their first lucid dreaming experience after about three months' time. Preparing for your first lucid dream involves an entire process, so there are many other steps you need to take first, before you are ready to have your first lucid dream. That's why it might take a regular person a while before they are able to enjoy lucidity while dreaming.

In order for a beginner to induce their first lucid dream, they must become familiar with certain mental exercises, and practice meditation, visualization, and dream intention. At the same time, they need focus, determination, and a strong will. The process requires effort and commitment, and you need to be consistent with your practice, if you want to increase your number of lucid dreams and enhance your experiences.

Lucid dream inducing methods

Dream Recall

To start with, you have to work on your dream recall. What is this? Remembering your dreams. The easiest way to train yourself for this is to keep a dream journal. Have a notebook and a pen handy near your bed, and every time you wake up from a dream, make sure to write down everything you can remember; general things, as well as details. After all, the faintest ink is more reliable than the most powerful memory, and, when it comes to dreams, that goes double. If you don't write it down immediately, you run the very real risk of losing it forever. Timing is key here, so don't wait until morning, because you will forget it. Scribble it down as soon as you wake up.

When you start to remember your normal dreams, you are also able to identify patterns, themes, and signs that appear in those dreams. This can help you learn more about yourself, and about your unconscious mind. Make sure to continue with this exercise until you reach a frequency of at least one recalled dream every night, before you move on to try and induce a lucid dream.

Identifying signs that you are dreaming

This method relies on learning to identify signs that you are currently dreaming. Signs include anything that cannot happen in real life, such as flying, for example, meeting a historical figure, finding yourself in a past era, having green skin, etc. When you are able to train yourself to automatically identify the signs, you can recognize the fact that you are dreaming. This brings lucidity. It's a good idea to learn what these signs are in waking life, so it will be easier for you to identify them in your dream.

Naps

One of the most effective methods of inducing a lucid dream is napping. It has been proven that lucidity often occurs when one takes a nap during the day, but you can also increase your chances of having a lucid dream in the morning. How do you do this? Well, you have to wake up earlier than usual, say, an hour earlier, stay awake during this time, and practice meditation or think about lucid dreaming. Then, allow yourself to fall back asleep, and now your chances of having a lucid dream will have increased as much as 20 times.

The explanation for this is that you were conscious for a while, and when you fell asleep again, your conscious brain will still be engaged within the dream. Now is the time to firmly establish lucidity, and tell yourself that you are, in fact, dreaming, which helps ground you, and offers you control over your lucid dream. Lucid dreaming is also known to occur when your sleep suffers interruptions at night, like waking up suddenly, or being awake for a while before slipping back into your slumber.

MILD (Mnemonic Induction of Lucid Dreams)

MILD is one of the most well-known techniques for lucid dream induction, and it consists of setting yourself up to recognize that you are dreaming. You are essentially training yourself to remember that you are in a lucid dream the next time you have one. This is good to do after you wake up from a dream, and intend to go back to sleep, right after you've written down the details of your previous dream.

The first step is to try to recall your dreams as vividly and as accurately as you can. Next, before falling asleep again, repeat your intention of recognizing that you are dreaming, over and over again. Think of it as a mantra and really focus on it and its meaning. Now, recall your previous dream and try to identify when you realized you were dreaming, and thus, woke up. Learning to recognize what induces lucidity in your dreams is very valuable information that you should have. Now imagine that you are dreaming, you identify the sign that indicates that you are in a dream, but you continue with it, successfully completing your plans or intention. Finally, continue doing this until you fall asleep, so that you can ensure your intention is clear and that you will remember it.

Testing Reality

Again, this method is all about repetition in waking life. Choose something that you can do to test whether or not you are experiencing reality or a dream. You know how they say you should pinch yourself? This is similar, only more reliable, because it is actually possible to feel pain in lucid dreams. All you have to do is write something down on a card or a piece of paper and take it with you wherever you go.

Then, try and look at it as frequently as possible, but at certain times. Say, when you remember something about your dream, when you arrive home, when you talk to a certain person, etc. Every time you look at the paper, see what happens with the letters. Are they the same? Do they spell the same thing, or does the word change? Look away and then look at the paper again. Do this a couple of times. If everything is the same, you are not dreaming, but if the word changes or the letters look strange or illegible, you are most likely lucid dreaming.

Another thing you can do is visualize a dream while you are awake. Close your eyes and imagine the scenery, the sounds, and what you can smell, or see in front of you. Visualize the entire world around you, as well as what you are doing or wish to be doing. Also think of anything that might be strange or out of the ordinary in your dream world, like colors that are off, laws of physics that are no longer working, etc. You have to focus as hard as you can to feel like you are in a dream.

Now, imagine you are doing something in a dream; something particularly dream-like, like climbing up a volcano, fighting aliens, traveling to the center of the world, etc. Whatever you would like to experience in your next dream, make sure to visualize it while imagining that you are dreaming.

Chapter 4 – How Can You Stimulate Lucid Dreaming or Assist Lucid Dreaming via Technology, Drugs, or Supplements?

Technology for lucid dreaming

This is a little known fact, but there are certain devices that can assist people in their lucid dreaming endeavors. They are completely safe and thoroughly researched in different laboratories, so there is no need to feel apprehensive about using them. For a beginner, the most difficult thing is managing to remember their intention and that they are dreaming. For this, they need a reminder. This is something these devices can help with, by providing this reminder via flashing lights, which will not disrupt or interfere with your dream or your REM sleep.

You know how sometimes there is a sound in real world, like music or a crying baby, a rooster or an alarm clock, and you incorporate the noise into your dream as coming from an entirely different source? These devices operate similarly, by introducing sounds and lights into your dream. The sounds are necessary, because some people are heavy sleepers and don't notice the lights cues. When going into the dream, you have to remember that when you see the lights and hear the sounds, those are cues that you are dreaming. This will trigger your lucidity.

Some versions of the devices allow you to alter the intensity of the lights according to your requirements, so they can be filtered into your dreams and become noticeable, but not cause you to wake up. You can also practice in your waking life, so you can identify the cues while you are immersed in the dream. In addition, the device can also detect eye movement. This is useful to identify your REM sleep stage, so it can introduce the cues at the right time, in order to trigger lucidity.

The need for learning to identify the cues in your waking life is because they might be incorporated in a covert way in the dream. It is possible for the lights to interfere and just flash in front of your eyes, but it is also possible for them to become part of the dream, via something like ambulance lights, lighting, fluorescent lights, etc. In a case like this, it is very easy for you to fail to recognize the cues and not give them a second thought.

It has been reported by people wearing the device that certain buttons meant to disable cues don't work during nighttime. What happened? They tried pushing the button, and it failed to make the distinct sound. However, to their surprise, they found out that it wasn't that the device was defective, but they were actually *dreaming* that they had woken up and tried disabling the device. This is called a false awakening, and it sometimes happens to lucid dreamers. If this happens to you, next time, take it as a sign that you are dreaming, to help you hold onto your lucidity.

Keep in mind that devices meant to help with lucid dream induction do not create lucid dreams for you on demand. The device cannot make you have a lucid dream. It can; however, assist you in your quest for lucidity, by providing you with the aforementioned cues, through lights and sounds, meant to indicate that you are currently dreaming.

Because lucid dreaming is such a personal thing, it can be difficult to pinpoint exactly what the rate of effectiveness for such a device is. There are so many factors that come into play, from each person's REM sleep, and finding cues that do not disturb the dream, to their ability to identify cues and recognize that they are in a lucid dream.

However, even considering these sometimes elusive contributing factors, it has been documented, without a doubt, that lucid dream inducing devices help increase the frequency of lucid dreams, and that the cues actively encourage their occurrence. Especially when used in tandem with a method, such as MILD (Mnemonic Induction of Lucid Dreaming), the results are overwhelmingly positive.

So the takeaway from this should be that while devices cannot make you have a lucid dream experience, they do accelerate and encourage the process. Lucidity is stimulated and triggered by a device's cues, and this leads to more lucid dreams than you would normally have.

Supplements for lucid dreaming

Over the years, there have been suggestions that certain types of medication could encourage lucid dreaming. But whether it's about prescription medication or simple vitamins, the effect is more likely due to the placebo effect. Because lucid dreaming is very susceptible to your strong belief and conviction, it makes sense that if you think a supplement will stimulate your ability to dream lucidly, then it most likely will.

Certain drugs are known to alter your REM sleep in ways which could lead to a higher frequency of lucid dreams, but it could also very well produce nightmares. Among them are alcohol and marijuana, as well as various LSD-related drugs. However, the majority of them are illegal in most places, and administration without medical supervision is not recommended, anyway.

Chapter 5 – What Is It Like to Dream Lucidly?

If you've never experienced a lucid dream before, you're probably wondering what it feels like to be in one. Well, for starters, it is nothing like your average dream. It's like stepping into a different world, a magical realm, if you will, where everything is possible, and events are fuelled by your desires and personal fantasies. As soon as you become aware that you are dreaming, you are basically being awoken to this alternate reality, where you have control over your actions, and sometimes, the actions of others. Anything can happen and anything you want can come true as soon as you wish it.

It's worth noting that normal, real-world laws do not apply in a lucid dream. Laws of physics are ignored, as well as social rules and mores, and all experiences are significantly more intense than in a normal dream, because of your awareness. Each lucid dream will be unique in its own way, even if you actively try to recreate a previous one.

Sensory experiences

Of course, in dreams you also perceive everything differently than in real life. This is because, unlike waking life, the information is not perceived through your five senses (taste, sound, smell, sight and touch), and then manipulated accordingly by your brain, but instead, directly projected by the brain, through your imagination and memory. This way, you are able to feel everything as intensely as in waking life. Here's what a few sensory experiences feel like in lucid dreams:

Flying

Yes, it is possible to experience something you never have before, via lucid dreaming. While most of us have flown in an airplane before (or maybe even a helicopter), I can say with some certainty that no one has ever flown without any kind of machine. Unless they're Superman, but that doesn't count, now does it?

Flying in a lucid dream can be scary, but so incredible. You're able to glide over skyscrapers, hills, and mountains and see the world from up above. The people look small and ant-like, rushing to whatever business they have, while you look on. There's a distinct feeling of weightlessness and freedom that you experience and it truly is unlike anything else.

However, you have to be really careful with awareness when it comes to flying, because whenever you lose lucidity, there is the risk of falling. That is because you forget you are dreaming, and thus, that the experience is not real, but imaginary, and you suffer the typical "consequences" you would in real life.

Eating

Eating in a lucid dream is every bit as good as doing so in real life. Actually, no, scratch that. It's *better*. Why? Because while the food tastes just as delicious, it won't have any unpleasant effect on your digestion, weight, health, or appearance, so you can enjoy chocolate ice cream to your heart's content.

Also interesting? The fact that you can totally try dishes you've never actually had before. This is possible because your brain relies on your expectations for things with which you have no real life experience to draw from. If something looks yummy, it will probably taste yummy, and if you expect something to taste disgusting, it will. So really, you ultimately control everything, even when it comes to food, and the best part is that every bite is as good as the first. Mmmm.

Pain

Pain is, indeed, something you might get to experience in a lucid dream, and it's, well... it's not exactly pleasant. Things that hurt in real life will also hurt in your dream, like, say, bashing your head into a wall, but you may also find yourself in a situation you've never actually experienced before, such as being shot, or some other scenario where pain is inflicted upon you. This is also going to hurt due to the same reason why you can "taste" foods you've never tried: expectations. You expect it to hurt if you're being hanged or shot in the leg.

But while the pain seems very real, it's not, and it can be instantly stopped by simply thinking about something else, moving onto another activity, or removing yourself from that situation. In addition, you won't be worrying about healing your wounds, treating yourself, permanent damage, medical expenses, and all the other real-life factors that make the situation worse. It's still not a pleasant thing to experience in a lucid dream, and it may be more frequently related to a lucid nightmare, but it still beats being in real-life pain.

Emotional Experiences

I mentioned earlier in the book that your experiences may vary in intensity. This happens in accordance to the activity you are currently partaking in and how it makes you feel. Your feelings will be overwhelmingly positive ones, with the negative only occurring in nightmares.

In fact, you might even become *overexcited*, which sounds good and certainly *feels* good, but is not ideal for a seamless lucid dreaming experience. You see, when you get super excited because you've achieved lucidity, you are more likely to wake up, and that's not what you want, right? You have to pay attention to this, at least in the very beginning, when people are usually prone to these kinds of emotions.

But the important takeaway is that you can control your emotions in a lucid dream; you just have to remember to remain calm in the face of overwhelming excitement. With time, you will get used to it, and it will become less likely for you to lose your focus.

Learning about Yourself

One of the most valuable experiences you can have while dreaming lucidly is getting in touch with your inner self. You can learn a lot about yourself and your hidden fears, desires, and even personality traits. Sometimes, our own motivations seem to be hidden from us; that's because they come from our unconscious minds, and we are not aware of them in waking life. But in lucid dreams, they can be revealed, as long as we ask the right questions.

Yes, you can question your dream self about pretty much anything that's on your mind, but you have to be prepared for answers that may be more honest than you are willing to hear. Your questions can trigger some intense experiences that you can definitely learn from, so ask them carefully.

Cognitive experiences

Control

Many people think that control is gained through simple awareness, but that is not true. Control does not come with lucidity, or not total control, anyway. Basically, you have control over your own self, your movements, and your actions, as well as your environment, which you can change according to your own will. However, other people present in your lucid dream will still act independently, along with all other figures, including animals.

Control is tricky, because you can lack it altogether, it can be partial, or it can be more present. It all depends on you; on your will and on your level of awareness and lucidity. For example, you will not be able to control major parts of your dream if you are only partially aware. For more control, you need to have excellent focus and strong willpower; otherwise you will not be successful.

You have to keep in mind that you will not be able to control every single aspect and detail of your dream, nor will you be aware of everything around you. Your focus will stay on the things that are in your immediate vicinity, or rather, right in front of your eyes. So don't expect to be able to control the texture of the leaves or other such details in your dream world.

On the other hand, once you practice lucidity, your possibilities are endless. You can do everything you've ever wanted, as long as you *believe* that you can. Again, expectations stand at the core of the issue here, and they are what ultimately set the parameters of what you can and cannot do in your dream.

Awareness of Past, Present, and Future

It probably won't come as a surprise that your dream self is not preoccupied with distant memories of the past, or what's going to happen in the future. Dreams, in general – and lucid dreams are no exception – focus on the now. The present is all that matters, and memory doesn't really factor into the dream world in any way.

You can attempt to remember things from the real world or from the dream itself, but you either won't be very successful, or you will have to concentrate very hard on the task. Because memories are hardly and rarely relevant in the dream world, there is no need for them. This is also because our brains are not able to access them successfully during our sleep hours.

You will probably also find it difficult to remember your dreams upon waking, which is why it is best to write them down as soon as you wake up, when all the details are still fresh in your mind. Otherwise, you might be faced with losing the memories of the dream forever.

One instance when you need to make use of your memory is when you are actively trying to remember your dream's intention. When you set out to have a lucid dream, you have to prepare in advance. This means you need to have a rough idea of what you want to dream about, in what kind of universe you want to be, where you want to go, and how to get there. Of course, you don't need to figure out every single detail – that takes the fun out of it – but it's good to know what you are trying to achieve in this particular dream experience.

This requires some sort of plan that you can visualize beforehand, and attempt to remember later, when you are already immersed in the dream world. It won't always work and you will sometimes find yourself in the environment you envisioned, but without being able to remember what you were supposed to do in this setting. This can be frustrating, but have no fear; even if you have no idea what you're doing, you're still in for a hell of a ride, provided by your imagination and your unconscious mind.

Awareness of Surroundings

You already know that the dream world is considerably different than the real one in almost every way. You, yourself are different in this projected world, and so is the way you perceive the things around you and the way you think. Or better said - the way you *don't* think or the things you don't think about. Like your surroundings, your location, or your purpose.

In real life, you have a sense of location, from the geographical one, to your immediate surroundings, and you are aware of who you are, what you are, and what your general purpose in the world is.

In the dream world, however, all these things are irrelevant. The dream world is a different realm, where none of these things come into play. Things are not as sharply divided; they're not black and white. Instead, they are a lot hazier and often unfamiliar, but that's ok. If you found yourself in an unfamiliar location and situation in real life, you would probably become worried, or even panic, in some cases. But not in lucid dreams! In them, you are only concerned with the things in front of you or around you, with no regards for the "outside" world, about whose existence you are implicitly aware.

Chapter 6 – How Do I Control My Dreams?

The theory is good and all, but you are probably wondering (rather impatiently) how you can actually control your dreams. Is there any practical advice I can give you? Any secrets I can share? Foolproof techniques that can help you get your way every time? Well, actually, yes, this is something I can help you with. You see, there are some methods you can employ to control certain aspects of your dreams. They can range from more general to very specific, and will prove to be immensely helpful in learning how, exactly, you can control your lucid dream.

Dream Control Methods

Time Travel

The most obvious way to time travel in a lucid dream is via a time machine, of course. All you have to do is get in and set it for the time and place where you want to end up. Remember that you really have to believe that it will work in your dream, and be able to visualize what it will look like. Just press some buttons and voila!

Alternatively, you can try flying way up into the sky, until you can't see anything beneath you. The ground below should disappear under the clouds. Now, just visualize both the place and the time you want to go to, and then return to the ground. The world should now be transformed, according to your wishes and expectations.

Flying

Flying is obviously a very popular dream request and desire, and it's probably one of the first things most of us attempt to do when we have our first lucid dreams. However, even though it's a common wish, it can be difficult to control for a beginner, because it is so egregiously out of place in the real world.

You run the risk of falling, because you don't entirely believe you are able to fly. Again, it's all about your own confidence, and strong belief in your abilities. If you believe you can fly, you can. If you're convinced you will fall, you will. It's very simple, really. Telling yourself you can until you succeed may not always work in real life, but it definitely works in lucid dreams.

To make it easier for you to start off, consider employing assistance of some sort, like an umbrella, a balloon, wings, or anything of the sort. You can also start small, by jumping around, and getting higher with every attempt. This should help you build confidence in your flying abilities, and eventually, you will be able to fly without any trouble at all.

Introducing Objects

If it is a specific object you are after, all you need to do is visualize it. However, it won't just appear before you, you have to find it. No, not like playing hide and seek, but rather looking for it in hidden places like a pocket, a box, a hole, a drawer, behind a corner, or even behind your back. An obvious option is to go straight to the source and look for something you want in the place where you are most likely to find it. For example, go home to find your mom, go to the library to find a book, etc.

Scenery Changes

Because things don't just magically appear in front of your eyes – and this includes your environment – you will have to find an alternative way to instantly change the world around you. There are some tried and true techniques that can provide help in this situation:

- Turn your back, visualize the new setting, and then turn around to find everything changed to your specifications.
- Step through a door, and instantly travel to another setting.
- Change the TV channel and step into the TV world.

- Start spinning and visualize a completely different world when you stop.
- Go through a portal to another world, or a different dimension; usually one that looks like a mirror.

As long as you really believe and expect things to happen your way, you will be successful in making virtually anything happen inside your lucid dream.

Meeting Figures

In lucid dreams, you can meet just about anyone, which is a fascinating feature for most people. This can be your chance to "summon" a deceased loved-one, talk to a celebrity, exchange ideas with a historical figure, or whoever else you desire. Keep in mind that they are still projections of your own self.

You can make anyone appear by just visualizing them, and then turning around or turning a corner. Expect the person to be there and they will. You can also "ask" the dream to materialize someone, and it doesn't have to be a specific person, either. For example, you could wish to be shown the person you will marry, yourself in a number of years, or other people from the future.

Addressing Your Unconscious Mind

I've mentioned that in a lucid dream, you can have the fascinating experience of talking to your own unconscious mind, and receiving answers that will provide very valuable insight into the way your mind works. It may seem strange, and a little intimidating to directly talk to your inner self, but it can be done.

The easiest way to achieve it is to project your unconscious mind on another figure in your dream. You can imagine them as a person (or as an animal, why not?) and ask them everything you're curious about. Just be prepared for answers that might blow you away.

Maintaining Dream Control

As you now know from previous chapters, it is essential to maintain complete lucidity if you desire strong control over your dream. It requires excellent focus and determination, otherwise you will keep forgetting you are dreaming, and you will fall in and out of lucid dreaming throughout your experience. So how *can* you maintain dream control? Here are some methods:

- Create an intention before you go to sleep – having a dream intention will ensure that you know what you're there for and what you are trying to achieve. You might not remember your exact intention (it happens), but you will at least be able to remember some parts that you visualized beforehand, like the setting or certain activities. This way, you are not completely unprepared, and you have something lucid to hang onto.

- Constantly tell yourself that you are dreaming – this is a surefire way of making sure the dream doesn't "swallow" you, with no way of getting out. Reminding yourself that it is just a dream ensures that you maintain total control, because you know that you can do anything, and that it won't have the same consequences as real life. When you forget, you allow the dream to take over, and put you in situations you do not desire.

- Acknowledge lucidity – this is something you have to do from the very beginning, before you have a chance to be carried away by the dream, and give your unconscious mind the opportunity to take over. Making a simple gesture like stating out loud that you are dreaming, or looking at your hands up close can help you acknowledge and establish lucidity.

Few beginners know this, but in a lucid dream, you can actually either control it, or simply remain passive and observe. Both options have their merits and both are certainly very interesting. But while control is more about fun and having new experiences, observation is skewed more towards asking questions and gaining insight. Whatever you opt for, make sure to maintain lucidity.

Maintaining Lucidity

But how do you manage to remain lucid, and thus, prolong your lucid dreaming experience? Especially in the beginning, your dreams are not going to be very long. Most likely, they are going to end after a few seconds, as soon as you realize that you are lucidly dreaming, and wake up. There are some things you can do to make sure that next time you are having a lucid dreaming experience, you don't ruin it by losing your grip on self-awareness.

- Pinch yourself or do something that will otherwise indicate clearly to you that you are dreaming. Think of it as a reality check of sorts that is meant to keep you grounded.

- Remain calm and try not to get overexcited at the prospect of lucid dreaming. This is a rookie mistake, and it can take you out of the dream immediately. Instead, relax and try to enjoy the dream, and take it further, without too much outward joy.

- Use your brain to solve a simple equation or something, in order to "awaken" your conscious mind.

- Move your body, like rubbing your palms or something. This engages the brain and manages to ground you, by making you aware of your body in your dream.

- Focus on achieving clarity. Say it out loud, if you have to, and your wish will be granted.

- Falling on your back can also help, because you are moving your body, and it can trigger something like a fake awakening. You fall back and "wake up" in bed, except you are still dreaming. But be careful; however, because it might also awaken you for real.

- Do a close-up of your hand, or observe the details of some other thing, thus maintaining lucidity.

- Awareness can also be brought on by spinning. However, this can also serve to change the setting of your dream, so be careful, if you are not ready to move on quite yet.

- But by spinning, you might also feel – or think you feel – your body moving in bed. Simply try to remain grounded, by telling yourself that this is your dream body, and not your real one. You are in a dream. Focus on creating a new dream scene. If you do wake up, don't be disheartened; you can go back into the dream. Just remain perfectly still and go back to spinning; imagine it. Now focus again on the next dream scene, and you might just be able to go back to dreaming lucidly.

Conclusion

I hope this book was able to help you learn all about lucid dreaming and taking control of your dreams.

The next step is to apply everything you've learned, and continue to learn even more things about lucid dreaming. Anyone can become a lucid dreamer; it is a total myth that you have to be some sort of initiated guru in order to be able to do it. All you need is some guidance, and someone to teach you how you can achieve this state of lucidity during your nightly dreams. Luckily, this e-book can answer your questions, and serve as your initiator into the fascinating world of lucid dreaming.

Allow the book to act as your personal guide to lucid dreaming, and follow its explanations and tips, in order to be able to gain control over your dreams. It does not have to be a difficult process, but like everything else, there is a learning curve to it. As long as you are genuinely interested and stick to it, there is no reason why you shouldn't be able to achieve lucidity.

Don't be afraid of the unknown. Instead, embrace it, and learn something new about yourself. This new experience can open you up to a whole new world of enhanced creativity, control, and deep knowledge about yourself, and your unconscious mind. We all have hopes, fears, and desires we are not aware of and that stay hidden, but you can tap into them and learn what drives your dreams. It is truly a fascinating process, and you can learn all about it from this e-book.

If you've always wanted to gain control over your dreams, or learn what it is that fuels your bizarre nighttime experiences, you can now gain valuable insight, thanks to this book about lucid dreaming. It's ok to be curious about it and to want to try it; the secret is to have someone show you the ropes, and prepare you properly for this unique experience of figuring out your mind.

Lucid dreaming has fascinated many people over the years. Many have tried and many have failed, because they were not able to benefit from the right kind of help. Thankfully, you will not be confronted with that problem, because this e-book is the answer to your questions regarding lucid dreaming. Let it be your guide, to teach you how to properly achieve lucidity, and insight into your unconscious mind and hidden personality.

THANK YOU!

If you liked this book, why not leave a review on Amazon? Being an independent publisher on the ever-growing eBook market, every review you post helps us reach more people and provides us with important feedback to better serve you and other readers in the future.

Also, don't forget to join the Lean Stone Book Club. It's the best way to stay up-to-date with all our books, activities and promotions. Furthermore, you'll get various opportunities to contribute to our book club (and even get rewarded for it).

>>>www.leanstonebookclub.com<<<

Thank you once again for reading our book! All our kudos go to you!

LEAN STONE
BOOK CLUB

Printed in the USA
CPSIA information can be obtained
at www.ICGtesting.com
CBHW071726051224
18501CB00007BA/303